Ancient
Roman
Warfare

By Rob S. Rice

Please visit our Web site at www.garethstevens.com
For a free color catalog describing Gareth Stevens Publishing's
list of high-quality books call 1-800-542-2595 (USA)
or 1-800-387-3187 (Canada).

Library of Congress Cataloging-in-Publication Data

Rice, Rob S.
    Ancient Roman warfare / by Rob S. Rice.
        p. cm. — (Ancient Warfare)
      Includes bibliographical references and index.
      ISBN-10: 1-4339-1974-5   (lib. bdg.)
      ISBN-13: 978-1-4339-1974-9   (lib. bdg.)
  1. Military art and science—Rome—History—Juvenile literature.
2. Rome—History, Military—Juvenile literature. 3. Military art and science—
History—To 500—Juvenile literature. 4. Military history, Ancient—Juvenile literature.
I. Title.
U35.R528   2009
355.020937-DC22   2009006201

This North American edition first published in 2010 by
GS Learning Library
1 Reader's Digest Road
Pleasantville, NY 10570-7000 USA

Copyright © 2010 by Amber Books, Ltd.
Produced by Amber Books Ltd., Bradley's Close
74–77 White Lion Street
London N1 9PF, U.K.

Amber Project Editor: James Bennett
Amber Designer: Joe Conneally

Gareth Stevens Executive Managing Editor: Lisa M. Herrington
Gareth Stevens Editor: Joann Jovinelly
Gareth Stevens Senior Designer: Keith Plechaty

Interior Images
All illustrations © Amber Books, Ltd., except:
AKG Images: 6 (Erich Lessing), 24; Art Archive: 22 (Gianni Dagli Orti/Musée du Louvre, Paris), 25
(Alfredo Dagli Orti/Museo della Civilta Romana Rome); Niels Bosboom: 16; Bridgeman Art Library:
23 (Museo e Gallerie Nazionali di Capodimonte, Naples); Corbis: 17 (Nathan Benn), 21 (Michael
Kooren/Reuters); De Agostini: 20 (G. Nimatallah), 27 (J.E. Bulloz); Fotolia: 4 (iamtheking33)
David Friel: 12; Steven Fruitsmaak: 14; Matthias Kabel: 19r; Stockxpert: 29 (Pippa West); TopFoto: 3, 28
(Print Collector/Heritage Image Partnership)

Cover Images
Front Cover: Left, Roman soldier's helmet (Dorling Kindersley); top right, equestrian statue of Marcus
Aurelius (Danilo Ascione/Dreamstime); bottom right, gladiator's shield (Gary Ombler/Dorling
Kindersley)
Back Cover: Center, parchment (James Steidl/Dreamstime); right, Roman soldiers (Amber Books)

Printed in the United States of America

1 2 3 4 5 6 7 8 9 13 12 11 10 09

Contents

Building an Empire

Rome began as several villages around the Tiber River in Italy in 753 B.C. Over time, the Etruscans, a people who lived in central Italy, conquered Rome. They ruled the city until 509 B.C.

Romans disliked living under the Etruscan kings, so they rebelled. After the rebellion, Rome became a **republic**, or a state with elected leaders.

Romans soon conquered other cities. Over centuries, the Romans built a huge empire.

As the empire grew larger, it needed stronger leadership. Powerful **emperors** ruled the Roman Empire beginning in 27 B.C.

The Roman Empire lasted for more than 2,000 years. Part of its success was due to its well-trained army. But Romans made strides in other areas too, such as engineering. Roman aqueducts brought fresh water for drinking and bathing. The Romans also invented the arch to support strong bridges and multi-storied structures.

▼ HEART OF THE EMPIRE
The forum in Rome was the place where Roman citizens went to discuss business, daily events, and to hear their leaders speak. There were temples surrounding the forum where the Romans could worship their many gods.

Building the Army

Many years before the empire was formed, Romans needed an army to protect their growing territories. At first, all male Romans served in the military. Every five years, the republic had a **census** to count its male **citizens** to learn which position each man would fight.

Young men reported each year for training. Officers organized the soldiers into divisions called centuries, which had between 60 and 100 men. Sixty centuries were called a **legion**.

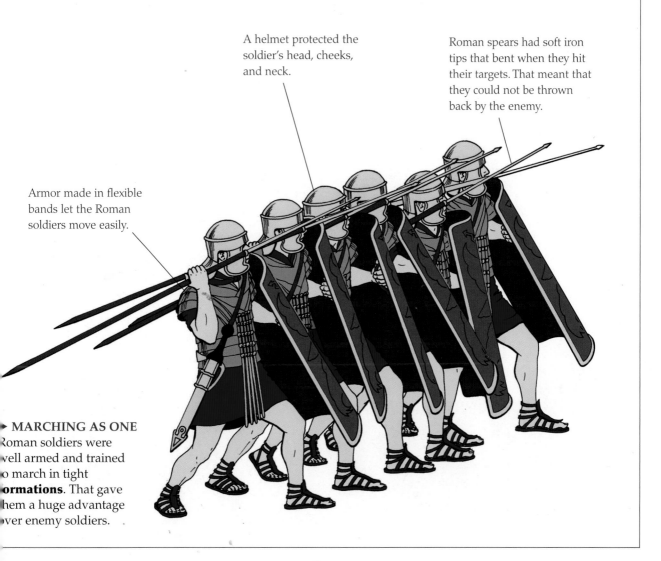

A helmet protected the soldier's head, cheeks, and neck.

Roman spears had soft iron tips that bent when they hit their targets. That meant that they could not be thrown back by the enemy.

Armor made in flexible bands let the Roman soldiers move easily.

▶ MARCHING AS ONE Roman soldiers were well armed and trained to march in tight **formations**. That gave them a huge advantage over enemy soldiers.

SARCOFAGO CON
BATTAGLIA FRA ROMANI E DACI

Each man's wealth defined what weapons and equipment he could buy, and in which part of the army he served. After fighting, soldiers returned to farming or other jobs.

In 309 B.C., Gauls, invaders from the north, defeated the Roman army, burning Rome. The Romans never forgot that they had been defeated. They did not want it to happen again, so they improved their army. Some Romans became professional, paid soldiers who did nothing but fight.

Bring Your Own Horse

Roman soldiers who wanted to fight on horseback had to supply their own horses. Most could not afford horses, so Rome had few mounted soldiers. The small number of men who owned horses were called **equites** (EK-wit-tays). They had great power, as they were important to the army and government. Years later, soldiers were given horses and paid to fight as **cavalry**.

◀ **ROMANS VERSUS BARBARIANS**
This sculpture shows a Roman soldier fighting a **barbarian** tribe. The Romans called all foreigners barbarians because they thought that their strange languages sounded like the Greek phrase for the barking of dogs, *bar-bar-bar*. We still use the words *blah blah blah* to mean speech that cannot be understood. The Romans' training and equipment helped them defeat invaders.

In Their Own Words

"For I myself am a man with authority, and I have soldiers under me. I tell this one, 'Go,' and he goes, and that one 'Come,' and he comes. I say 'Do this' to my servant, and he does it."

—A Roman centurion, quoted in the New Testament, 1st century A.D.

Army Officers

Equites played an important role in the Roman army and government. All **senators** were equites. They made decisions for all Roman citizens. Ordinary people had no power in ancient Rome.

Officers who commanded the centuries were **centurions** (sent-YOUR-ee-onz). The centurions lived and fought with the men and kept order in the ranks.

Rome Expands

To increase its influence and territory, Rome formed partnerships with other cities. Some people from those cities joined the republic. They became Roman citizens. In other cases, land was conquered by force. Those lands became part of the empire. They had to be defended against Rome's enemies.

Rome fought a series of wars with the powerful north African city of Carthage between 264 and 146 B.C. Those were the Punic (PUNE-ic) Wars. The Romans protected Sicily, an island off the coast of Italy, defeated the Carthaginians, and conquered land as far away as Spain and Africa.

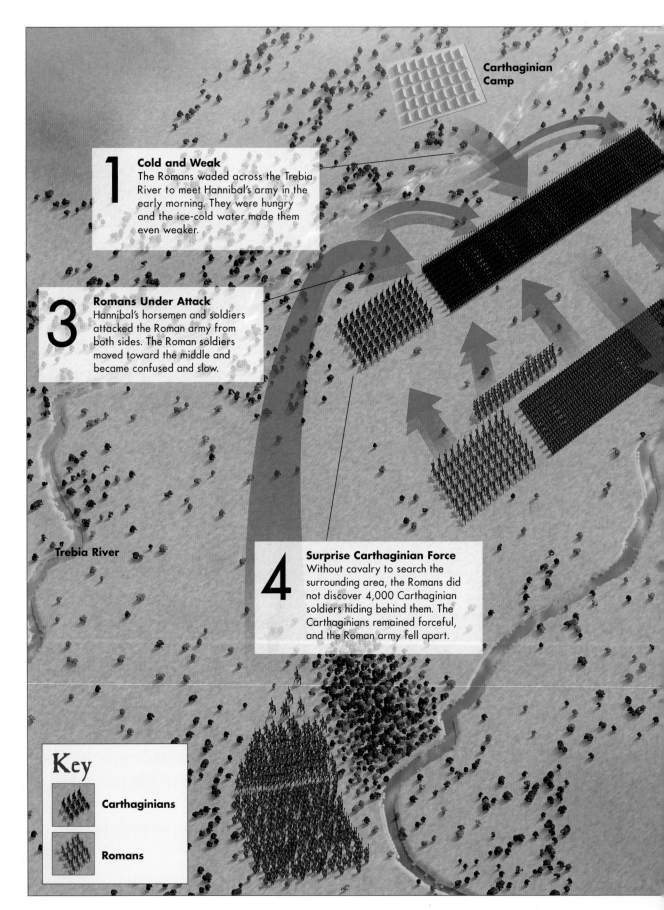

Carthaginian Camp

1 Cold and Weak
The Romans waded across the Trebia River to meet Hannibal's army in the early morning. They were hungry and the ice-cold water made them even weaker.

3 Romans Under Attack
Hannibal's horsemen and soldiers attacked the Roman army from both sides. The Roman soldiers moved toward the middle and became confused and slow.

Trebia River

4 Surprise Carthaginian Force
Without cavalry to search the surrounding area, the Romans did not discover 4,000 Carthaginian soldiers hiding behind them. The Carthaginians remained forceful, and the Roman army fell apart.

Key

Carthaginians

Romans

Po River

2 **Elephants Cause Panic**
Hannibal's elephants appeared out of the winter fog. The Roman horses ran away in fear, taking their riders with them.

Roman Camp

5 **A Terrible Defeat**
Only 10,000 Romans smashed through Hannibal's army and escaped. They were the only Roman survivors.

The Battle of Trebia

218 B.C.

Rome's greatest enemy was the Carthaginian general Hannibal. After Rome had defeated Carthage in 241 B.C., the Romans broke their peace treaty with Carthage and took more land. Hannibal swore revenge.

In 219 B.C., from his base in Spain, Hannibal ordered the attack of Saguntum, in Roman-occupied Spain. After, he led his army on African elephants over the Alps and into Italy, beginning the Second Punic War.

In the winter of 218 B.C., the two armies met. Some 35,000 Roman soldiers and horsemen faced 30,000 Carthaginians near the icy Trebia River.

Hannibal let the Roman army wade into the river. He knew this would weaken them. Then Hannibal's army attacked the Romans from both sides. His elephants frightened the Roman horses. Only 10,000 Romans survived Hannibal's trap—the rest were killed.

CHAPTER 2

Weapons and Equipment

The Romans had an organized army made up of foot soldiers called **infantry**. The largest unit in the army was a legion. Rome had two leaders, known as **consuls**, who were elected by the senate. At first, each consul commanded only one legion. Years later, during the Roman Empire, consuls commanded several legions at once.

Roman Legions

Early Roman soldiers used long spears. They fought in a big mass called a **phalanx**. As soldiers required greater

The Roman shield, the **scutum** (SKOO-tum), was very strong but heavy. The soldier rested it on his head to help support its weight.

▶ IN TRAINING
This group of Roman soldiers is training together. The Romans called this formation the **testudo** (tes-TOO-doe), or turtle. The Romans used the testudo when their enemies were shooting arrows at them. The walls and roof of shields protected the group like a turtle's shell.

The Roman soldiers wore heavy sandals called **caligae** (KAL-ee-guy) to protect their feet in battle and when they were marching.

protection, they also carried small swords and **javelins**, light spears that could be thrown great distances. Roman foot soldiers protected themselves with shields, helmets, and heavy armor.

Legions were organized into three lines. The first line was made up of soldiers who attacked the enemy directly. The second line was made up of more experienced soldiers. They switched places with first-line soldiers if they became tired or hurt. They also replaced soldiers who were killed. The legion's third line was reserved for highly skilled soldiers. Third-line soldiers were armed with heavier spears.

DID YOU KNOW?

The Romans knew that a man could only fight for a few minutes before he became tired. Roman soldiers were trained to switch places with each other. That enabled tired soldiers to rest and wounded soldiers to be rescued.

Special soldiers carried **standards** into battle. Those were signs that told of the battles the soldiers had won and the medals the unit had earned. The soldiers gathered around it in combat.

A centurion gave orders to the men under his command.

helmets. Members of the cavalry traveled ahead of the army to locate and watch the enemy. They also chased off enemies.

During a battle the cavalry fought enemy horsemen to keep them away from foot soldiers. The cavalry also pursued enemy troops who ran away, chasing them and killing as many as possible.

Cavalry were sometimes assigned to a specific legion. They were divided into groups of just over 500 men and operated on the sides, or flanks, of the legion.

Roman Weapons

Roman weapons were sturdy. If the Romans discovered that their enemies had more advanced weapons than they did, the

Foot soldiers who could not afford the equipment required by the legion were **velites**. Those men made up the light infantry. They kept watch so the legion was not attacked by surprise. The legions were also helped by foreign troops sent by Rome's allies, or friends.

Roman Cavalry

Roman soldiers who fought on horseback were called cavalry. Like the legionaries, mounted soldiers also wore armor and

▲ ROMAN CAVALRY
This man is taking part in a modern reconstruction of a Roman battle. He is dressed like a Roman cavalryman. He is wearing **chain mail** armor and carrying a long sword.

Romans quickly copied those designs. They were often inspired by foreign inventions, which they set out to improve. From the Gauls, the Romans copied chain mail, a type of armor made from small iron rings that were linked together. Chain mail protected soldiers from cuts and stab wounds.

Romans took the design of their helmets from an enemy tribe from Italy, the Samnites. The Romans also learned how to forge steel swords while fighting the Spanish and Carthaginians in Spain.

Over time, Roman shields became stronger and heavier. Later shields had flat bottoms so that soldiers could save their strength by resting them on the ground.

The Romans made short, heavy javelins to throw at close range. They also made

longer, lighter javelins to throw greater distances. The javelins were held together with wooden pegs that broke apart at impact. That kept the enemy from using those same javelins as weapons.

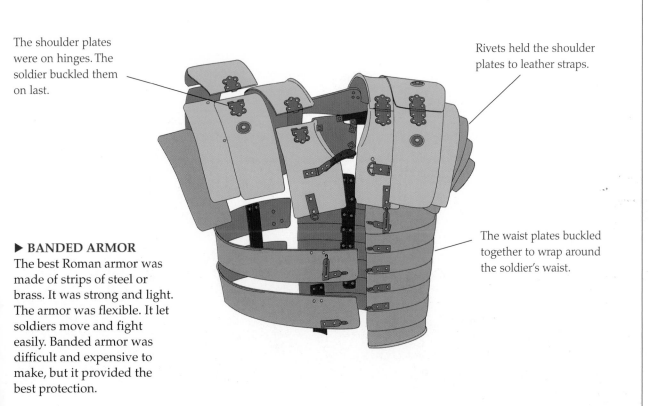

The shoulder plates were on hinges. The soldier buckled them on last.

Rivets held the shoulder plates to leather straps.

▶ **BANDED ARMOR**
The best Roman armor was made of strips of steel or brass. It was strong and light. The armor was flexible. It let soldiers move and fight easily. Banded armor was difficult and expensive to make, but it provided the best protection.

The waist plates buckled together to wrap around the soldier's waist.

CHAPTER 3

Roman Camps

The Roman army was organized, both in the field and in their camps. Camp doctors, engineers, and blacksmiths traveled with the army. Doctors kept wounds clean. They treated injuries quickly. Engineers ensured that the campsite had clean water for drinking and washing.

▼ ROMAN FORT

The Romans defended their borders on the edge of their empire. One of those borders was Hadrian's Wall, in northern England. Along the wall the Romans built forts for their soldiers. This is their fort at Chesters. The square buildings in this photograph are the remains of soldiers' living quarters. Down the middle of the street ran a trench which acted as a sewer.

DID YOU KNOW?

The battle of Cannae (216 B.C.) was the worst defeat in Roman history. Fifty-five thousand Romans were killed by Carthaginian troops under Hannibal's command. Hannibal was a clever general. Only two years earlier he had tricked the Romans into letting themselves get surrounded by his forces.

Blacksmiths repaired soldiers' weapons and armor. Soldiers built roads to move troops quickly. Along those roads, they built **fortresses** to protect important places. All Roman soldiers were trained to pave roads and build fortresses.

Building the Camps

Roman armies marched 18 miles (29 km) each day. When the troops stopped, the soldiers built that night's camp. The camps were always the same, so soldiers always knew where to find the kitchen and **barracks**.

Camps were rectangular, with ditches around the outside. All camps were protected by ditches and earthen walls. Building the wall was hard, but it meant that the soldiers had a safe place to defend if they were attacked during the night.

The Roman commanders slept at the center of the camp, where two main paths formed a cross. There was a gate on each wall surrounding the camp.

Permanent Camps

Some Roman camps became permanent forts, protected by stone walls. The soldiers built barracks, stables, a hospital, storage rooms, and other stone and wooden buildings. Permanent camps were comfortable living spaces. They had heated baths, large stores of food, and other supplies.

The horn, called a **cornu**, fitted around the man's shoulder. It had a low, buzzing tone that could be heard for miles.

The Romans believed their ancestors wore wolf skins into battle. This man wears a wolf skin to remind other soldiers that they are fighting for Rome, just like their ancestors.

▶ ROMAN SIGNALMAN
This signalman carries a brass horn, like a modern bugle. He would stand near the general and blow his horn to signal orders to the army. He wears armor and carries a sword in case he has to fight.

Laying Siege

Sometimes Roman soldiers surrounded a town, trapping everyone inside. Before long, those who were trapped ran out of food and risked starvation. This method of fighting was called laying siege. During the height of the Roman Empire in 52 B.C., Julius Caesar trapped his enemy, Vercingetorix (Ver-sin-GET-ur-icks), and an army of Gauls inside a town called Alesia.

Caesar built two walls around the town, and camped between them. One wall kept Vercingetorix and his army inside Alesia, and another protected the Romans. Vercingetorix and his men starved until they were forced to give up.

Roman watchtowers like this one were built from solid wood to protect soldiers from wind and rain. They had to be tall so the sentries could see as far as possible.

Burning torches were placed in metal holders to warn Roman soldiers of attack.

Soldiers stood on catwalks like this one to see across the surrounding countryside.

▶ A ROMAN WATCHTOWER
To defend the borders of the empire, the Romans built towers like this one so that **sentries** could keep watch. If they saw or heard anyone near the wall, the sentries would blow on horns, light fires, or beat drums to warn soldiers at nearby forts.

In A.D. 70, Jewish rebels captured the fortress of Masada, which was a part of the Roman Empire in Israel. The strong fortress was located on a high cliff. The Romans got in by building an earthen ramp all the way up to its walls. The Romans captured the fortress by using a **siege tower**. They pushed the tower up the ramp and used it to get over the fortress walls.

▼ A FAMOUS FORTRESS

King Herod of Judea built his palace at Masada to protect him from his own people. After Herod died, Jewish rebels took over the empty fortress. The Roman army surrounded it with fortified camps and built a huge siege ramp up to the walls. Evidence of the Roman camp and the ramps the soldiers built to reach the fortress are still there today.

CHAPTER 4

War at Sea

Early Romans were better fighters on land than at sea. During the first sea battles the Romans tried to ram and sink enemy ships with their boats. Another tactic was to crush the enemy's oars, preventing their escape.

When the Romans first fought the Carthaginians at sea, they were defeated. The Carthaginians were excellent sailors and they had been fighting at sea for centuries. The Romans needed new tactics to defeat their enemies at sea.

The eagle was the symbol of Roman power and the Roman Empire. Both enemies and allies recognized the symbol.

▼ A ROMAN WARSHIP
This **galley** is the kind the Romans would have used during the Punic Wars. It was rowed by almost 200 men. Special soldiers called **marines** stood on the top deck ready to board enemy ships and capture them. At the bow is a boarding bridge to let the marines cross over, and a ram to sink other ships.

The Roman commander was protected by this wooden tower during the battle.

The steering oar worked like a modern rudder.

A Secret Weapon

The Romans built new ships, adding a weapon called the **corvus** (crow), which was a movable wooden bridge. It was attached to the mast by several pulleys, with an iron spike sticking out underneath like a bird's beak.

When an enemy ship came close, the Roman crew dropped the spiked end of the corvus down on it. The spike held the

DID YOU KNOW?

Roman short swords were ideal for close combat on ships. When an enemy lifted his arm up to swing his sword, a Roman soldier was trained to stab him in the chest to kill him quickly.

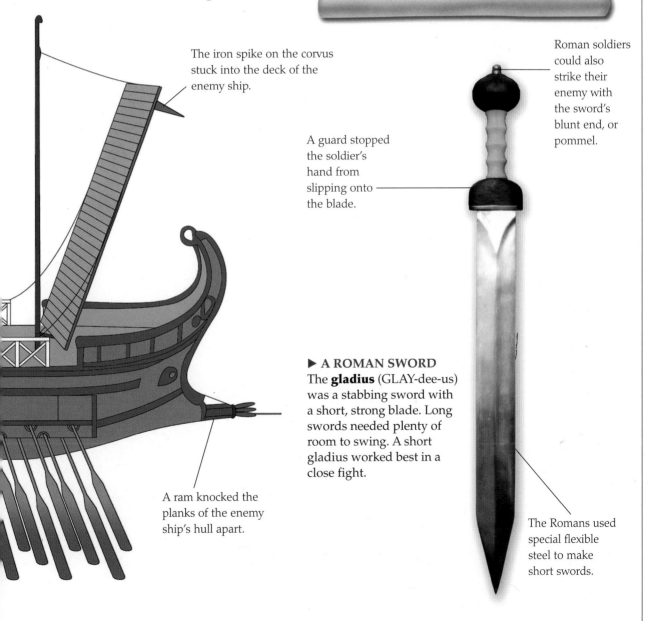

The iron spike on the corvus stuck into the deck of the enemy ship.

A guard stopped the soldier's hand from slipping onto the blade.

Roman soldiers could also strike their enemy with the sword's blunt end, or pommel.

A ram knocked the planks of the enemy ship's hull apart.

▶ **A ROMAN SWORD**
The **gladius** (GLAY-dee-us) was a stabbing sword with a short, strong blade. Long swords needed plenty of room to swing. A short gladius worked best in a close fight.

The Romans used special flexible steel to make short swords.

▼ READY FOR BATTLE

This stone carving dating from about A.D. 100 shows a row of marines standing ready on the deck of a Roman warship as it rows into battle. The rowers below them sit on two levels. The eye on the front of the ship was a good luck symbol. It was meant to help the ship to find its way home.

ship in place while Roman soldiers charged over the bridge.

Fighting on a ship's deck was more like fighting on land. Once Roman soldiers got onto the enemy ship, they were better able to defeat their enemies.

Allies and Pirates

Between 215 and 190 B.C., the Roman Empire grew larger. The Romans fought several sea battles against the Greeks and other kingdoms of the Mediterranean. Each battle won increased Roman territory. The Romans were helped by their allies, such as the Rhodians from Rhodes, an island off the coast of Turkey.

▲ THE "BONES" OF A SHIP
This is the remains of a small Roman ship from about A.D. 100. It was discovered buried in the Netherlands, near the Roman Empire's northern territory. Small ships were used to protect Rome's borders from barbarians.

In 67 B.C., the senate gave Pompey the Great, a consul and military leader, a special task. He was ordered to defeat the pirates who had been stopping shipments of food from crossing the Mediterranean to Italy. The Rhodians convinced Pompey that he should capture and control the ports where the pirates sold the stolen goods. Within four years, Pompey had mostly cleared the seas of pirates.

Canals and Swift Cruisers

In 37 B.C., the Roman leader Agrippa wanted to make a safe shipyard for his ships. To do so, he turned Lake Avernus in southern Italy into an inland harbor. Agrippa cleverly connected the harbor to the sea by a manmade canal. The canal could be easily defended against attack, so his ships were much safer than if they had been in a regular port.

Agrippa used fast, lightweight ships called **liburnae**. They were about 109 feet (33 meters) long and could be rowed by two rows of oarsmen. Those ships patrolled the seas by covering great distances quickly.

CHAPTER 5

Roman Leaders

Roman generals did not go to school to learn how to fight. Instead they studied the greatest commanders from earlier times and learned by example. The five ancient Romans profiled in this chapter are just a few of those leaders known for their military achievements. Their actions inspired other Romans throughout history.

Total Power

Early Romans disapproved of kings, but they knew that one person had to be in charge to protect the city. At times of crisis, the senate gave high-ranking Romans **imperium**, or total authority, to set laws and command an army. The commander of a legion was granted imperium so that he could give orders.

Consuls always had imperium. In an emergency, the Roman senate appointed one man as **dictator**. He had power over everyone else. Later in Rome's history, the emperors ruled as constant dictators.

◄ TRAJAN
Rome's greatest military ruler was Marcus Ulpius Trajan (A.D. 53–117). He defeated Rome's most powerful enemy, the Parthians, and conquered Dacia. Today Dacia is known as Romania after its Roman rulers.

HISTORY OF ROMAN WARFARE

500 B.C.	400 B.C.	300 B.C.	200 B.C.	100 B.C.
509 End of Etruscan rule	**460** Cincinnatus made dictator.	**309** Rome sacked by Gauls.	**202** Battle of Zama	**107** Marius reforms army.
		218 Battle of Trebia		

Cincinnatus

Lucius Quinctius Cincinnatus (sin-sin-AH-tus, 519–430 B.C.) was a Roman politician. In 460 B.C., he retired as consul to run his farm. Two years later, the Romans fought the neighboring Aequi people. During a siege, the Roman army became trapped in the hills, but a few horsemen escaped to Rome to tell the senate. The senate quickly appointed Cincinnatus as dictator, giving him absolute power.

Cincinnatus left his farm and rushed to Rome. He led an army into battle and defeated the Aequi, rescuing the trapped Roman soldiers. After solving the crisis in just 16 days, he resigned as dictator. Cincinnatus' swift resignation of authority was seen as a trait of good leadership.

Scipio the Elder

Scipio the Elder, or Scipio Africanus (236–183 B.C.), came from a long line of military leaders. Scipio's father and uncle were earlier Roman commanders who had been killed by Hannibal's men during the First Punic War. In 211 B.C., Scipio the Elder was given control over the Roman army in Spain. After several victories, Scipio was elected to consul in 205 B.C. to lead the Roman army in Africa. Scipio wanted to defeat Hannibal. He was angry that

DID YOU KNOW?

The memory of Cincinnatus not only inspired Romans. Cincinnatus was also a hero to the first U.S. president, George Washington. Like Cincinnatus, Washington refused to keep power any longer than he thought he had to. The city of Cincinnati was named after Cincinnatus as a way of honoring Washington's ideals.

▶ SCIPIO THE ELDER
Scipio employed clever tactics to defeat Hannibal. He trained his men to sidestep Hannibal's elephants when they charged. After, the soldiers regrouped and attacked the enemy from the sides and rear. Troops in those positions were less well armored.

70 B.C.   60 B.C.   50 B.C.   40 B.C.   30 B.C.   A.D. 100

67 Pompey begins his campaign against pirates.

52 Siege of Alesia

36 Agrippa defeats Sextus Pompey.

44 Death of Julius Caesar

31 Battle of Actium

70 Siege of Masada

101–106 Trajan's Dacian campaign

▲ FIERCE FOES
The Romans lost two armies to the invading German tribespeople shown on this stone carving from around
A.D. 200. The Germans were tough fighters and outnumbered the Romans. Once Marius had trained his army in
new tactics, Rome could defeat the Germans.

Hannibal's army had killed his father and uncle, and he wanted to avenge their deaths. But the Roman army needed better weapons. Scipio gave his soldiers new swords. He improved the javelin. He also studied Hannibal's tactics.

Scipio launched an attack on Carthage in Africa. In 202 B.C., Scipio and Hannibal met in a battle at Zama, near Carthage. Hannibal had often defeated the Romans by attacking them from behind. At Zama, Scipio used Hannibal's tactics against him. Scipio ordered his cavalry to surprise Hannibal's army from behind. Scipio led the Romans to victory, ending the Second Punic War.

Gaius Marius

Gaius Marius (157–86 B.C.) was a Roman army officer and political leader. After leading many Roman victories, Marius created the first professional Roman army. He recruited men without money or property and paid them to fight. Like Scipio, Marius gave his men better weapons and armor and trained them well. He made them carry so much during marches that his men earned the nickname "Marius's Mules."

In 102 B.C., two fierce and powerful German tribes invaded northern Italy and moved south toward Rome. Marius took his army north and fought two battles against the invaders. He defeated the Germans and returned to Rome in triumph. Marius' soldiers' loyalty had resulted in a swift victory.

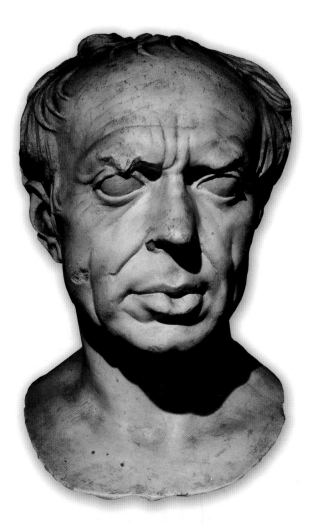

▲ MARIUS
Marius was the first Roman leader to allow men without property to serve as soldiers. They were more loyal to their generals than to Rome itself. Eventually they fought on the streets of Rome to make Marius the emperor.

In Their Own Words

"[Marius] got his soldiers into shape and order in the field by long marches, running, and by making every man carry his own kit and cook his own food."

—Plutarch, a Greek historian,
writing about Marius in A.D. 75

Agrippa

During the last days of the Roman republic, before it became an empire, much fighting took place between the Romans themselves. Many leaders competed for power and control. That was especially true during the leadership of Julius Caesar, who was killed by assassination in 44 B.C.

Before Julius Caesar died, he handed over power to Marc Antony and Octavian.

Marcus Vipsanius Agrippa (63–12 B.C.) was Octavian's son-in-law and close friend. He was a skilled commander. Agrippa ended rebellions and founded colonies throughout the empire.

As a military leader, Agrippa was called on to control Sextus Pompey, the son of Pompey the Great. Sextus Pompey had occupied Sicily and wanted to seize power over the entire empire. To overpower

▼ **HEIGHT OF AN EMPIRE**
Over many years, the Roman army defeated enemy after enemy and took their land. The Romans conquered most of Europe and North Africa, and a large part of the Middle East.

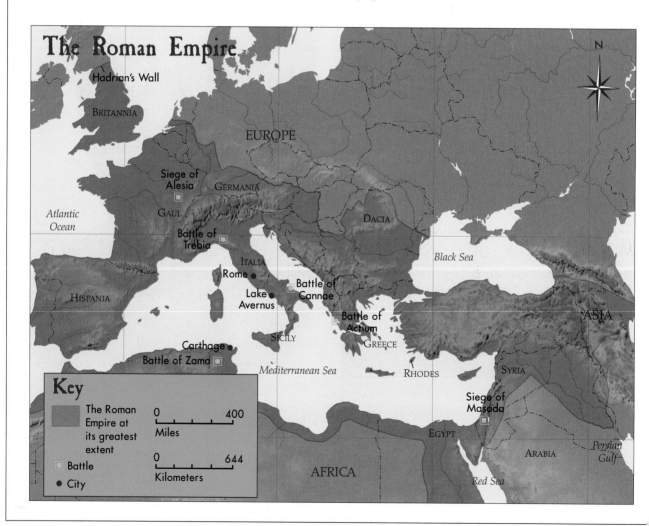

▼ AGRIPPA
When Octavian became emperor, his friend Agrippa defended Rome's borders and kept peace throughout the empire. That gave Octavian time and money to rebuild the city.

In Their Own Words

"Every one of Antony's ships had three or four of Octavian's around it, the crews jabbing with spears, javelins, poles, and flame weapons, which they tossed into the enemy. Antony's ships had catapults, too, and fired bolts down from towers. Agrippa extended his line to get past the side of Antony's."

—Plutarch, writing about the battle of Actium in 31 B.C.

The Battle of Actium

In 31 B.C., Agrippa's navy trapped Antony and Cleopatra's warships in the Gulf of Actium, in Greece. Antony and Cleopatra had gathered a fleet of 500 ships and an army of 70,000 men. Agrippa had the 400 ships he had used to drive off Sextus Pompey, and he marched his army of 80,000 overland into northern Greece to stop Antony.

Antony's ships tried to build up speed so that they could sail through Agrippa's formation. Instead, Agrippa attacked the moment they left the bay. Agrippa's medium-sized vessels surrounded Antony's ships. Antony and Cleopatra escaped on the flagship, while most of the fleet surrendered.

Agrippa's victory made his friend Octavian Rome's first emperor. Agrippa was celebrated and made consul by Octavian for three terms. During that time Agrippa reformed the Roman system of taxation and created a system of roads throughout the empire.

Octavian and Marc Antony, Sextus Pompey had built a strong navy. But Agrippa also built a powerful fleet and destroyed Sextus' navy in a sea battle off the coast of Sicily in 36 B.C.

Meanwhile, Antony had started a relationship with Queen Cleopatra of Egypt. Both rulers wanted to defeat Octavian so that they could take over the entire Roman Empire. But the great commander Agrippa was loyal to Octavian.

Trajan

Marcus Ulpius Trajan (A.D. 53–117) was born in Roman-occupied Spain. He spent most of his life fighting in the Roman army. After many victories, Nerva, an old general who had been chosen to be emperor, adopted Trajan. Trajan was made Nerva's **heir**. When Nerva died, Trajan became his successor. Trajan became one of Rome's most admired emperors.

From A.D. 101, he launched a series of attacks on the kingdom of Dacia, now Romania. His army defeated the Dacian army, and he returned to Rome triumphant.

Trajan then led many successful military campaigns throughout the region now known as the Middle East. Those campaigns expanded Roman territory until the empire stretched from Britain to the Persian Gulf. To mark his achievements, the people of Rome built Trajan's Column in his honor, a monument standing 125 feet (38 meters) high.

▼ **WAVES OF BARBARIANS**
This section of Trajan's Column in Rome shows the Roman cavalry fighting barbarians in Dacia. The carvings are 625 feet (190 meters) long and show more than 2,500 figures.

▲ A RECYCLED MEMORIAL
The last great Roman emperor was Constantine I (A.D. 272–337) who held power from A.D. 324 to 337. This is the arch he built as his monument. We know that Constantine took stone and marble carvings from older memorials to decorate this arch. That was because Rome was no longer wealthy or powerful enough to have skilled artists and sculptors. The Roman Empire was in decline.

End of an Empire

The successful Roman government and military systems became models for future civilizations. As time passed, however, the empire grew too large and hard to manage. Roman territories frequently came under attack. Roman armies were overburdened. Foot soldiers could no longer fully defend Roman borders. Romans also fought among themselves, further crippling their power. Eventually, outsiders captured Rome, and the once successful Roman Empire crumbled.

Glossary

barbarian—a word used by ancient Romans to describe foreign enemies

barracks—buildings used to house soldiers

caligae—heavy sandals with leather binding, worn by Roman soldiers

catapult—a machine powered by tension, used for throwing objects

cavalry—soldiers who fight on horseback

census—an official count of people

centurions—professional officers in the Roman army

chain mail—flexible armor made from many tiny metal rings linked together

citizens—members of Roman society with certain rights and privileges. Women and slaves living in Rome were not citizens.

consuls—the highest elected officials in the Roman republic

cornu—a brass horn used to broadcast signals to Roman troops during battle

corvus—a movable wooden bridge on board a ship, with an iron spike on the underside, used for boarding enemy ships

dictator—a person given sole power for a limited period in order to deal with an emergency

emperors—the rulers of the Roman Empire between 27 B.C. and its fall in A.D. 476

equites—senior officers in the Roman army who fought on horseback and were high-ranking members of society

formations—arrangements of troops

fortresses—well-defended military camps or fortified towns occupied by soldiers

galley—a long, low warship powered by oars

gladius—a short, stabbing sword used by Roman soldiers

heir—the person who will inherit a high-ranking position on the death of its holder

imperium—power granted to a person by the Roman senate that enabled that person to make laws and control the Roman army

infantry—foot soldiers

javelins—spears designed to be thrown by hand

legion—a Roman army division of 60 centuries, each made up of 60 to 100 men

liburnae—fast, light ships with two banks of oars and sails

marines—soldiers trained to fight from and on board ships

phalanx—a group of foot soldiers in formation, with shields overlapping and long spears held upright

pilum—a heavy javelin

republic—a state in which power is held by the people and which is governed on their behalf by an elected official or council

scutum—a curved, rectangular shield

senators—senior government officials in ancient Rome

sentries—soldiers whose job is to look out for enemies at a fortress or border post

sieges—attacks in which enemy cities or fortresses are surrendered by armies in order to capture them

siege tower—a tall wooden building on wheels that was placed next to the walls of a fortress to allow soldiers to climb up and gain entry more easily

standards—military flags or symbols carried on poles that displayed battles won by an army

testudo—a formation of Roman soldiers with shields held tightly together above their heads, used to defend against arrows and other missiles

velites—lightly armored foot soldiers who carried javelins

For More Information

Books

Ancient Rome. Technology in Times Past (series). Robert Snedden (Saunders Books, 2009)

The Ancient Romans. People of the Ancient World (series). Allison Lassieur (Children's Press, 2005)

The Best Book of Ancient Rome. Deborah Murrell (Kingfisher, 2007)

How to be a Roman Soldier. Fiona MacDonald (National Geographic Children's Books, 2008)

Life in a Roman Fort. Picture the Past (series). Janet Shuter (Heinemann Library, 2004)

The Roman Army: The Legendary Soldiers Who Created an Empire. Dyan Blacklock. (Walker Books For Young Readers, 2004)

Tools of the Ancient Romans: A Kid's Guide to the History & Science of Life in Ancient Rome. Tools of Discovery (series). Rachel Dickinson (Nomad Press, 2006)

You Are in Ancient Rome. You Are There (series). Ivan Minnis (Raintree, 2004)

Web Sites

Ancient Rome
http://www.kent.k12.wa.us/staff/DarleneBishop/ rome/Rome.html
Tour ancient Rome through photographs of its ruins, including the Colosseum, the Pantheon, and the city of Pompeii.

Kidipede: Ancient Rome
http://www.historyforkids.org/learn/romans
Learn more about the ancient Romans including fun facts about Roman engineering, inventions, art, and architecture.

The Roman Empire
http://www.roman-empire.net/children/index.html
Explore the Roman Empire in detail at this web site that includes maps of the empire and a drawing of a typical Roman house.

The Romans: The Roman Army
http://www.bbc.co.uk/schools/romans/army.shtml
Read more about the Roman army at this web site that includes facts about daily life, a glossary, maps, and a time line.

ThinkQuest: Empires
http://library.thinkquest.org/CR0210200
Discover ancient civilizations of the Romans, Greeks, and Egyptians. Click on "Ancient Rome" for fun facts and photos, as well as crafts and other online activities.

Publisher's note to educators and parents: Our editors have carefully reviewed these web sites to ensure that they are suitable for children. Many web sites change frequently, however, and we cannot guarantee that a site's future contents will continue to meet our high standards of quality and educational value. Be advised that children should be closely supervised whenever they access the Internet.

Index

About the Author

Dr. Rob S. Rice is a Professor in the Department of Naval History at the American Military University. He has a Ph.D in Ancient History from the University of Pennsylvania. He is the author of sections of several other books including the *Oxford Companion to American Military History*, *Battles of the Ancient World*, and *Battles of the Bible*.